...PLLEGE C...
...TION

About this book

Every year more than three million visitors flock to
see the Tower of London and its treasures. However,
when it was built by William the Conqueror nearly ten
centuries ago, it was not quite so popular. The English people saw the fortress as a symbol of foreign
conquest.

The Tower has had many uses over the centuries —
some of them surprising. It has housed a zoo, the
Royal Mint, the Royal Arsenal, the Record Office and,
of course, the Crown Jewels. As the most famous
prison in England it has housed, amongst others,
Anne Boleyn, Queen Elizabeth I, Guy Fawkes, Sir
Walter Raleigh and, in more recent times, Rudolf
Hess, Hitler's deputy. The Tower has also been the
scene of pageantry, execution and murder. Built as a
fortress, it has stood firm throughout its history —
despite fifteen direct bomb hits during the Second
World War.

The colourful, very exciting and sometimes bloody
history of the Tower is vividly brought to life in this
simply written book with seventy illustrations.

Some of the words in this book may be new to
you. You can look them up in the list on page 91.

AN EYEWITNESS HISTORY BOOK

The Tower of London

Anne Mountfield

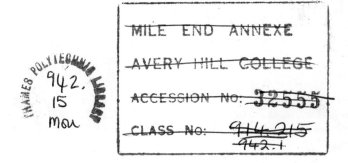

Wayland

More Eyewitness History Books

The Age of Drake
Animals in War
Beads, Barter and Bullion
The Changing Seaside
Children of the Industrial
  Revolution
Clothes in History
Country Life in the Middle
  Ages
The Firefighters
Florence Nightingale
The Glorious Age of Charles II
Greek Myth and Legend
The Horseless Carriage
Islam
Kitchens and Cooking
Livingstone in Africa
Markets and Fairs
The Mayflower Pilgrims
Men in the Air
The Monarchy
Newgate to Tyburn
Overland to the West

Pirates and Buccaneers
Popular Entertainment
The Printer and his Craft
The Railway Builders
Road Transport
Shakespeare and his Theatre
Ships and Seafarers
Shops and Shopping
The Slave Trade
Sport through the Ages
Stagecoach and Highwayman
Steam Engines
The Story of the Cinema
The Story of the Wheel
Street Cries
1066
Tom-tom to Television
Toys in History
The Tudor Family
Tutankhamun's Egypt
A Victorian Sunday
When Dinosaurs Ruled
Witchcraft and Magic

Frontispiece: View of the Tower of London

First published in 1979 by
Wayland Publishers Ltd
49 Lansdowne Place, Hove
East Sussex BN3 1HF, England

© Copyright 1979 Wayland Publishers Ltd

ISBN 0 85340 641 3

Phototypeset by Trident Graphics Limited, Reigate, Surrey
Printed and bound by The Pitman Press, Bath, England

Contents

1 Castle, Mint and Zoo

The Tower of London is, in fact, not one but many towers. High above them all stands the tallest, strongest and oldest tower. This is the Keep, or White Tower, which was built in 1078 by the Norman invaders.

The Norman tower was one of three fortresses built by the invaders to frighten and subdue the rebellious Londoners. It stood on the north bank of the River Thames to guard London against attack from rival Danish raiders.

The kings who came after William the Conqueror went on building the Tower. In the twelfth century Henry II and Henry III strengthened the defences of the Tower and it became a great castle, able to withstand siege, with towers for the archers and dungeons for the prisoners. It was also a working village, where bows and arrows, cannons and firearms were made, and where coins were minted. By the end of Edward I's reign in 1307 the Tower stood on an island, surrounded by a moat, with two portcullisses, three drawbridges and a huge watergate.

Many kings and queens of England stayed in the Tower before their coronation. They also kept their jewels and important papers there, and sometimes even their animals. Henry III built a palace there in the thirteenth century, but this was destroyed by Oliver Cromwell in the seventeenth century.

The picture on the opposite page shows the city of London in medieval times.

A ROMAN SITE. In this picture the artist shows
how the city wall of Roman London must have looked
about 700 years before the Norman invasion. You can
see how the walls ran along the river and then turned

sharply north into the city. These corner walls were
still standing at the time of the Norman Conquest in
1066. The Normans used them to protect two sides
of their first wooden fortress.

THE STONE TOWER. In 1078 the Normans began to build the Tower in stone. This model shows that the turret tops were cone-shaped at that time. The walls of the Keep were twenty metres high and five metres thick. The corners were faced with limestone shipped all the way from Caen in Normandy. The conquered Saxons were forced to drag the stone up from the river, build the walls and dig the ditches. Compare this model with the picture of the White Tower as it looks today on page 15.

GUNDULPH'S CHAPEL. Many of the stone buildings at this time were churches. A French monk, Gundulph, was chosen to take charge of building the Tower. Inside the Keep he built this beautiful Chapel of St. John. You can see the round Norman arches and the strong, plain pillars.

THE GHOST AND THE TOWER. Thomas à Becket was Constable of the Tower in 1161, before he became Archbishop of Canterbury. However, a quarrel broke out between Becket and Henry II over matters of religion and in 1170 Becket was murdered by the King's knights. When Henry III tried to build a gate tower at the lower of London, it fell down three times. People said that the ghost of Thomas à Becket had been seen, pushing it down in revenge. The picture opposite shows the murder of Thomas à Becket.

THE TOWER GROWS. In the twelfth century Richard I built a curtain wall round the Keep, and many new towers, to protect it against siege. This picture shows how it must have been built. You can see men climbing the wooden scaffolding. The poles were lashed together with rope.

ROYAL PALACE. This is Henry III, giving instructions to his architects. They are ready with set squares and compasses. Henry and his Queen, Eleanor of Provence, built a royal palace at the Tower with a Great Hall and richly decorated chapels. They spent over £10,000 — a huge sum in those days.

THE WHITE TOWER. As you can see, the White Tower is not very white today. It was given this name when Henry III ordered its walls to be whitewashed inside and out. Shiploads of black marble were used to decorate the inside. By the end of Henry's reign the Tower must have been a dazzling sight with its black and white rooms, gilded carving and glittering stained glass.

STRONGHOLD. The royal jewels were stored in the safety of the Tower and can still be seen today in the Jewel House. For many centuries important records and documents were also kept there. The Tower was also a great weapon store, where craftsmen made bows and arrows. Later, the Ordnance made firearms and stored gunpowder. Whoever controlled the Tower also controlled much of England's wealth.

THE ZOO. Henry III kept a royal menagerie at the Tower. He had three leopards, and a polar bear that fished in the Thames at the end of a rope. Louis IX, King of France, presented him with an elephant and Henry built an Elephant House for it. Sadly, it died within two years. The elephant and rhinoceros in the picture came to the Tower in 1686. The tradition of a royal zoo at the Tower which was open to the public went on until 1834 when it was moved to Regent's Park.

CRUSADER'S CASTLE. In the thirteenth century Edward I built an outer wall round the Tower. A new moat was then dug round the outer wall and the old moat was filled in. Edward, pictured here on his horse, had fought in the Holy Land in the Crusades. He had learnt much about castles from his travels abroad and made the Tower one of the strongest castles in Europe.

TRAITORS' GATE. Edward I built the enormous St. Thomas's Tower to guard the river entrance. Edward II later made a great arch in it, big enough to hold three modern double-decker buses. This huge gate, with its grim portcullis, became known as Traitors' Gate because so many prisoners passed through it when they came up the river to the Tower.

JEWS IN THE TOWER. These Jews are celebrating their feast of the Passover. Many Jews were traders and moneylenders at that time. They were often persecuted in the Middle Ages. In 1274 Edward I was told that the Jews were clipping the edges off coins and making money for themselves from the clippings. So he imprisoned 600 Jews in the dungeons of the Tower. Many died of disease and many more were hanged.

THE MINT. After the Jews were imprisoned, Edward I had a new pattern of coins made. Here you can see how it was done. A blank piece of metal was hammered between two 'dies'. The die had the pattern of the coin engraved on it. Edward brought the dies into the Tower for safekeeping, and set up a big Mint there. It was the only place in the country where gold coins were minted.

2 Peasants and Princes

The Hundred Years War began when Edward III claimed the throne of France. The English archers who set off to fight the French took with them long-bows from the workshops of the Tower of London. The English army was led by the Black Prince, Edward III's son. He sent many royal French prisoners to the Tower.

Edward III had seven sons, but he was followed as king by his grandson, Richard II. While the war with France dragged on, Richard had to face rebellion at home. The leaders of the Peasants' Revolt in 1381 were the only successful invaders of the Tower in all its history. They met with little resistance.

Richard II was later forced to give up the throne. His abdication was the start of a long family feud between two branches of Edward III's family, the Yorkists and the Lancastrians. Each side claimed the throne. This feud became known as the 'Wars of the Roses' because each side used a rose as their badge. In 1483 two famous victims of this quarrel came to the Tower. They were the young Prince Edward, heir to the throne, and his brother, whom you can see in the picture opposite. However, Edward was never crowned because his uncle declared himself king and the princes were never seen again. It is thought that they were murdered in the Tower, probably by their uncle. The Garden Tower where they lived became known as the Bloody Tower after their disappearance.

24

THE CORONATION OF RICHARD II.   It was the custom for kings to spend the night before their coronation fasting at the Tower. This was too much for Richard II, who was only eleven years old. You can see him above, fainting on his way to be crowned. Four years later, in 1381, Richard returned to the Tower to seek safety from the Peasants' Revolt, when rebel armies marched from Kent, led by John Ball and Wat Tyler.

THE BLACK PRINCE.   The picture opposite shows Edward, the Black Prince. In 1356 he led a triumphant procession through the streets of London bringing King John of France and his son, Prince Philip, as prisoners to the Tower. Their ransom cost France three million florins. Pedro the Cruel of Castile gave the Black Prince another treasure — a ruby. You can still see this ruby in the Imperial State Crown.

THE PEASANTS REACH LONDON. This picture shows Richard II in the barge which took him from the Tower to meet the rebels at Greenwich. His advisers would not let him land to hear the peasants' demands for lower taxes and greater equality. The next day, however, the king did meet some of the rebels at Mile End. While he was away, another band of rebels burst into the Tower. They 'lay and sat on the King's bed while joking', and asked his mother for a kiss.

WAT TYLER. The peasants dragged two unpopular ministers, Archbishop Sudbury and the King's Treasurer, from the Tower and executed them on Tower Hill. Richard agreed to meet Wat Tyler's men at Smithfield as you can see here. Fighting broke out, and Tyler was killed. The peasants trusted the king's brave offer: 'Let me be your leader', and went home. But the royal promises were soon forgotten and many peasants were hanged.

THE KNIGHTS OF THE BATH. It was a custom for kings to create new knights at the Tower on the eve of their coronation. Henry IV made a great ceremony of this. His forty-six new knights each took a bath as a sign of purity. That is why they were known as Knights of the Bath. After bathing and resting the knights spent the night in prayer in the Chapel of St. John.

CHARLES, DUKE OF ORLEANS. This famous picture of the Tower shows Charles, Duke of Orleans, who was captured by Henry V in the French wars. It is like a comic-strip: you can see several pictures of Charles riding to the Tower, arriving, and (in the cutaway part on the right) writing poetry inside the Tower.

THE MURDER OF HENRY VI. Henry VI was a religious and scholarly man, and not very interested in government. During his reign quarrels between the Lancastrians and Yorkists continued. Eventually he was deposed and put in the Tower by the new king, Edward IV. An ex-king in prison was too much of a threat, so Edward had him murdered. On the anniversary of Henry's death, lilies and roses are still placed in the Wakefield Tower. They come from King's College, Cambridge, and Eton College, both of which he founded.

THE UNCROWNED KING. This picture shows the young Prince Edward arriving in London with his uncle, the Duke of Gloucester, after the death of his father, Edward IV. He stayed in the Tower before his coronation, and his brother Richard joined him there as a playmate. Then their uncle declared himself king and became Richard III. For a while the princes, aged thirteen and ten, could be seen playing with bows and arrows on Tower Green. Then they disappeared, and were never seen again. It is thought that they were murdered by their uncle.

THE YEOMEN WARDERS. Henry VII set up a royal bodyguard, the Yeomen of the Guard. Later the guards at the Tower became known as 'Yeomen Warders' and wore scarlet dress uniform like that of the royal guard. It has the Tudor badge of white and

red roses together. 'Beefeaters', as they are commonly known, still live in the Tower to guard it and show visitors round. This photograph shows Victorian Yeomen Warders. In 1858 they were given a plain navy 'everyday' uniform.

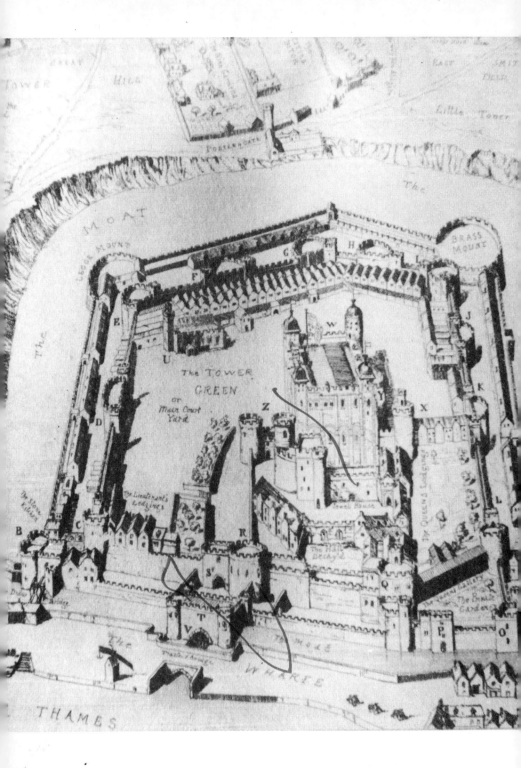

3 Off with their Heads!

When Henry VIII became king in 1509, he decided to use the Tower more as a stronghold and less as a royal residence. He strengthened the Tower, added new stocks of arms and two great semi-circular mounts for cannons. He also built the timbered Lieutenant's Lodgings, now known as the Queen's House, and rebuilt the Chapel of St. Peter ad Vincula which had been destroyed by fire. Many of the prisoners who were executed at the Tower during Henry VIII's reign were buried in this chapel. They included two of his six wives. Henry did not often keep his court at the Tower. After the execution of his second wife, Anne Boleyn, he never visited the Tower again. The plan of the Tower opposite shows what it looked like in 1553.

In 1534 Henry VIII broke with the Catholic Church in Rome because the Pope would not give him a divorce to marry a new queen. Henry then declared himself Supreme Head of the English Church in place of the Pope. Not everyone could accept this break and many died for their beliefs on the scaffold.

When Mary I, who was a Catholic, became Queen in 1553 she wanted her reign to be a peaceful one. However, many Protestants wanted Lady Jane Grey to be Queen, and so Mary was forced to imprison her in the Tower. Lady Jane was one of seven prisoners (five of them women) who were executed within the Tower, on Tower Green. Most executions took place outside the walls — on Tower Hill if the prisoner was important, or by hanging at Tyburn if not.

HENRY VIII. This is Henry VIII who is well known for having six wives. His first wife, Catharine of Aragon, did not give him a son. Then Henry fell in love with her pretty lady-in-waiting, Anne Boleyn. Henry wanted to marry Anne, but the Pope would not allow him to divorce his first wife. This quarrel led to a split with the Pope. Henry declared himself head of the Church of England, and made everyone swear their loyalty to him instead of the Pope.

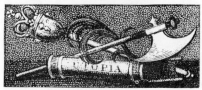

SIR THOMAS MORE. Sir Thomas More was Henry's Chancellor until the split with the Pope. Here you can see his Mace of Office lying beside his famous book, *Utopia*, and the axe which executed him in 1535. More was put in the Tower when he refused to recognize Henry as head of the Church. On the scaffold, More saw that the steps were shaky. 'See me up safe,' he said, 'and for my coming down – let me shift for myself!'

ANNE BOLEYN. Anne Boleyn's baby son died, but she had previously produced a daughter, who later became Queen Elizabeth I. But Henry tired of her. She was tried for treason and condemned to death.

She asked not to die by the axe: 'I have but a little neck,' she said. So a swordsman came from France to execute her. Ten days later, Henry married Jane Seymour, his third wife.

THOMAS CROMWELL. Thomas Cromwell was one of Henry VIII's powerful ministers. He helped found the Church of England and took charge of breaking up the monasteries and seizing their land and riches. You

can see him here with Archbishop Cranmer. They are presenting Henry with Cranmer's translation of the Bible into English. Cromwell fell from favour when he arranged Henry's fourth marriage to the ugly Anne of Cleves. In 1540 he was executed on Tower Hill. Henry then divorced Anne of Cleves and married Catharine Howard.

TOWER GREEN. The site of the scaffold on Tower Green always attracts tourists, yet only seven people are known to have been executed inside the Tower. It was thought an honour not to have a crowd looking on. Catharine Howard, Henry VIII's fifth wife, died on Tower Green in 1542. She admitted loving another man. 'If I had married the man I loved, instead of being dazzled by ambition,' she said, 'all would have been well.' In 1543 Henry married his sixth wife, Catharine Parr, who outlived him.

THE ORDNANCE. Henry built a new storehouse for guns and armour at the Tower. The picture opposite shows some of Henry's guns in use against the French. You can still see Henry VIII's suits of armour at the Tower. The later ones show how fat he became.

41

EDWARD VI. This is the coronation procession of Edward VI, Henry VIII's son, on its way from the Tower to Westminster in 1547. Edward was a sickly boy and died six years later. The Catholic Princess Mary was next in line to the throne. But some powerful people did not want a Catholic Queen and so Lady Jane Grey, Henry VIII's granddaughter, was proclaimed Queen. However, she only reigned for nine days and was then sent to the Tower.

THE COUNTESS OF SALISBURY. Next you can see the death of Margaret Pole, Countess of Salisbury. She was a devout Catholic. Her son, a Cardinal, had written a book condemning Henry's divorce. It was said that she refused to lay her head on the block. So she was clumsily hacked to death.

MARRIAGE AT THE TOWER. The new Queen, Mary 1, married Philip, the Catholic King of Spain. Here you can see the ceremony which took place in the Chapel of St. John at the Tower. Philip was not there, so an ambassador took his place. Many plots and rebellions began against the Catholic rulers who persecuted the Protestants.

WYATT'S REBELLION. The Spanish marriage was unpopular. Sir Thomas Wyatt led one rebellion against the Queen. This picture shows the attack on the Tower. Cannons from the Tower fired back at the Protestant rebels, destroying many homes across the river. Wyatt and hundreds of his rebels were arrested and later executed.

LORD GUILDFORD DUDLEY. Wyatt's rebellion led
to the trial of Lady Jane Grey and her young husband,
Lord Guildford Dudley. Both were condemned to
death. Dudley was imprisoned in the Beauchamp
Tower, and you can still see his sad carvings on the
wall: 'JANE . . . JANE'. One morning in February
1554, Lady Jane watched her husband go to his
execution on Tower Hill. Then she saw this dreadful
procession return with his dead body being carried
away for burial.

LADY JANE GREY. This picture shows Lady Jane on the scaffold later the same day. She had wept when she was declared Queen. She wept again at the terrifying sight of the executioner all in black. She was quickly blindfolded, and then executed.

ELIZABETH AT THE TOWER. In 1554 Mary's half-sister Elizabeth, the Protestant daughter of Henry VIII and Anne Boleyn, was brought to Traitors' Gate. She called to the crowd, 'I come in no traitor'. She was

kept in the Bell Tower and was allowed to walk along this stretch of the ramparts — Elizabeth's Walk. No evidence could be found against her. When she was released, church bells rang out all over London.

RELUCTANT REVENGE. When Elizabeth I became Queen in 1558, she returned to the Tower for three days of celebration before her coronation. For twelve years no executions took place on Tower Hill. Then support began to grow for the Catholic Mary Queen of Scots, and Elizabeth began to persecute the Catholics. Many priests and Catholic laymen were executed at the Tower. Here you can see some of the crosses and sacred hearts they carved on the walls to help their prayers.

ELIZABETH AND ESSEX. Queen Elizabeth never married but she had several favourites. One of them was Robert Devereux, Earl of Essex. He lost the Queen's favour when he married and was charged with treason. He was given the honour of a private execution on Tower Green. It took three strokes to kill him. Afterwards Elizabeth was often found weeping in the dark for him.

50

4 Gunpowder, Treason and Plot

When Queen Elizabeth died in 1603, she was succeeded by James I. His coronation procession started from the Tower, but it was very small for the Plague was raging in London, and crowds were not encouraged. James often visited the Tower and it was during his reign that the royal menagerie was housed in the Lion Tower. He enjoyed lion-baiting in the moat and setting dogs against the lions from the menagerie. At the Tower, he watched William Shakespeare act with the King's Company, and gave him cloth for a cloak as reward.

Religious disputes still brought prisoners to the Tower. Their heads were often set on spikes to rot outside it. James was the son of a Catholic mother, Mary Queen of Scots, but he was a Protestant. Many plots were hatched to put a Catholic back on the throne. On Bonfire Night children still remember the death of one such plotter, Guy Fawkes.

The reign of the next king, Charles I, ended in Civil War. Afterwards Oliver Cromwell, the Puritan general, became Lord Protector of England from 1653 to 1658 and there was no king for those five years. He melted or sold most of the Crown Jewels which had been kept at the Tower for centuries. In this chapter you can read the exciting story of how they were replaced, then stolen, then found again, in the reign of Charles II. The picture opposite shows the Tower in the seventeenth century.

THE GUNPOWDER PLOT. This group of Catholic plotters planned to blow James I and his Ministers to pieces at the State Opening of Parliament. A tip-off led to a search of the vaults of Parliament. Thirty-six barrels of gunpowder were discovered. So was a 'dark and desperate fellow', called Guy Fawkes. The date was November 5th 1605.

GUY FAWKES. Guy Fawkes was seized, as you can see here. He was put in the terrible 'Little Ease' cell at the Tower, which had no light and was so small that the prisoner could not sit or lie down. His shaky signature on the confession shows how cruelly he was tortured on the rack to make him reveal the names of his fellow conspirators. Many of the plotters, including Guy Fawkes, were hanged, and their heads were displayed on London Bridge.

TORTURE. The 'Scavenger's Daughter', shown opposite, was a common form of torture. It could squeeze a man until blood ran out of his fingertips. In Charles I's time, all this came to an end. John Felton, a prisoner at the Tower, claimed that torture was against the law. A Royal Commission agreed with him that 'no such punishment is known or allowed by law'. Instruments of torture became museum displays.

SIR WALTER RALEIGH. This picture shows the explorer, poet and courtier, Sir Walter Raleigh. He had been a favourite of Queen Elizabeth. In 1603 he was accused of plotting against James I and was imprisoned in the Tower. His family went with him, and a child was born in the Tower. Raleigh was allowed to use a shed in the Lieutenant's garden for his chemical experiments. He even tutored the Prince of Wales. In 1616 James I released Raleigh, then nearly sixty-five, to go to Guiana in search of gold. But he returned empty-handed and was executed in 1618.

THE DEATH OF STRAFFORD. Strafford was a loyal minister of Charles I, but he was not popular with Parliament. As a result of the king's quarrels with Parliament, Strafford was accused of treason. Parliament demanded his death when he was tried. Charles I

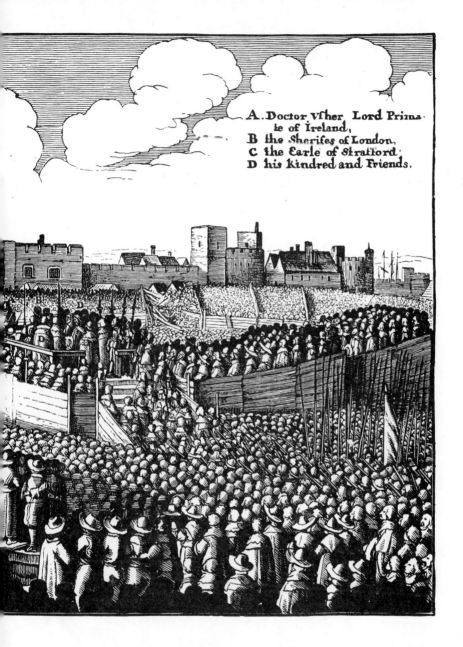

A. Doctor Vſher Lord Prima-
   te of Ireland,
B the Sherifes of London,
C the Earle of Strafford,
D his kindred and Friends.

wept as he signed the Act that sent Strafford to his death in 1641. This huge crowd of 100,000 people was sketched by an eye-witness, Hollar, who was the royal drawing master. In those days executions brought out crowds like modern Cup Finals.

ARCHBISHOP LAUD. In 1645 Archbishop Laud followed Strafford to the block. He was thought to be sympathetic to the Catholic religion. Here you can see the executioner showing the crowd his head, and shouting: 'Behold a traitor's head!' The scaffold was often covered with straw or sawdust to soak up the blood. The prisoner paid the executioner for his work. He might be given clothes or jewels in return for a quick death. Sometimes a bad executioner took several blows to kill his victim.

THE SALE OF THE CROWN JEWELS. Charles I was executed after the Civil War in 1649 and Oliver Cromwell was made Protector of the Commonwealth. Cromwell filled the Tower with prisoners and pulled down the Palace and Jewel House. Here you can see him with the Crown Jewels, said to date back to Edward the Confessor. He ordered most of them to be broken up and sold.

GENERAL MONK. This is the funeral procession of
General Monk. You can see his wife following the
coffin. She was the daughter of one of the five lady
barbers at the Tower, and was 'not at all handsome or
cleanly'. Monk met her when he was imprisoned in

DRUMS, FIFE, ETC.   TRUMPETS.   BLUEMANTLE.   THE STANDARD.

GREAT OFFICERS TO HIS GRACE.   BARONS.   BISHOPS.   EARLS.   SERGEANT
TRUMPET.

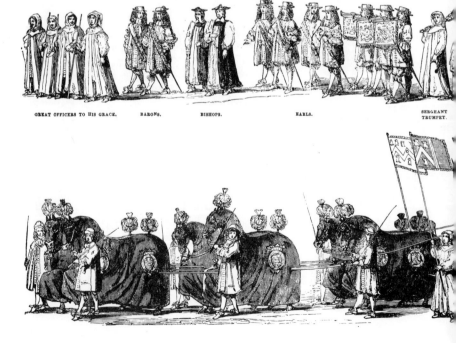

the Tower for fighting for Charles I. He was released to fight for Cromwell in Scotland. But in 1660 he helped in the Restoration of Charles II and was made Duke of Albemarle. He died in 1670 and was buried in Westminster Abbey.

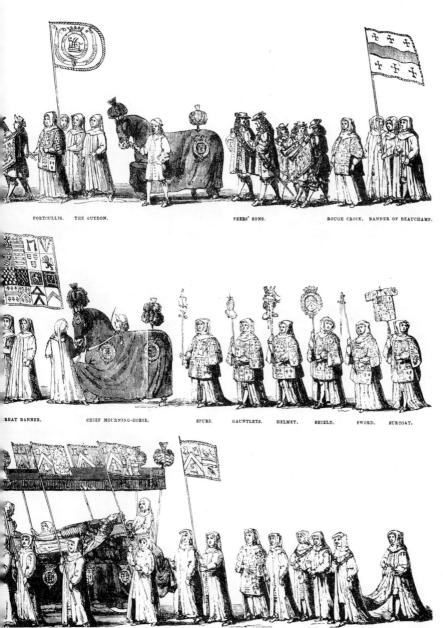

PORTCULLIS. THE GUYDON. PEERS' SONS. ROUGE CROIX. BANNER OF BEAUCHAMP.

BEAT BANNER. CHIEF MOURNING-HORSE. SPURS. GAUNTLETS. HELMET. SHIELD. SWORD. SURCOAT.

THE BODY. GARTER. CHIEF MOURNER AND SUPPORTERS.

THE COURT RETURNS. Charles II was the last king to stay at the Tower before his coronation. This picture shows his procession. He is carrying new Crown Jewels. Of the original Crown Jewels, only the

Ampulla, the Anointing Spoon and Queen Elizabeth's Salt Cellar had been saved by the monks at Westminster Abbey. So new ones were made, costing almost £32,000 – a vast sum of money in those days.

BURIED TREASURE.   This is Samuel Pepys, whose famous diary tells us a great deal about the Tower in Charles II's time. Pepys often visited the Tower and was even imprisoned there briefly. Part of the diary tells of his efforts to find treasure, said to have been buried in the Tower by Barkstead, Cromwell's Governor of the Tower. Pepys tried the cellars. He tried the gardens. The money has never been found. Barkstead, who 'looked cheerful' at his execution, took his secret to the grave.

THE CROWN IS STOLEN. This is 'Colonel' Blood, an Irishman who stole the Crown Jewels. Blood's nephew pretended he wanted to marry the daughter of Talbot Edwards, the Master of the Jewel House. Edwards showed them the Jewels. They then stabbed him and escaped with the Crown, Orb and Sceptre. Blood was caught within minutes, imprisoned in the Tower and then released and given a pension by the King. Many believed that Charles II was behind the theft, trying to get back the money the jewels had cost him!

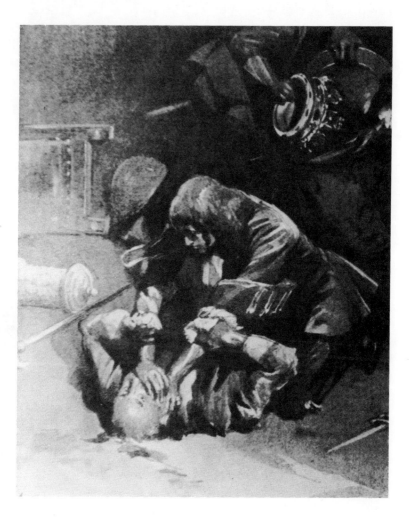

THE GREAT FIRE OF LONDON. This painting shows how near the flames of the Great Fire of 1666 came to the Tower. There was great danger that a

spark would cause a huge explosion at the Tower, and so the gunpowder stored there was quickly moved away.

MONMOUTH AND JACK KETCH. In 1685 the Duke of Monmouth tried to raise a rebellion against James II. The rebellion failed and Monmouth was put to death. This picture shows his execution. The executioner, Jack Ketch, took six blows to chop his head off. In 1683 Ketch took five blows to sever another head, and blamed the prisoner for not keeping still!

THE SEVEN BISHOPS.   Here you can see the Arch-bishop of Canterbury and six other bishops arriving by boat at the Tower in 1688. They had quarrelled with James II, who tried to bring back the Catholic faith. Crowds cheered the popular bishops from the river's edge and from boats.

5 Scientists, Soldiers and Spies

From the end of the seventeenth century the Tower was rarely used as a State prison. It became more and more important as a place of work, housing the Ordnance, the Mint and the Record Office.

The first Astronomer Royal, John Flamsteed, used a turret of the White Tower as his observatory until he moved to Greenwich in 1675. In 1695 two other famous men came to work at the Tower: the scientist and mathematician, Sir Isaac Newton, and the architect, Sir Christopher Wren.

Over the years the number of prisoners dropped to a handful. The axe grew rusty with disuse. The cannons of the Ordnance became outdated. The Mint moved away in 1810. The Zoo went to Regent's Park in 1834, though some London visitors were tricked into believing it was still at the Tower. They bought tickets to see 'The Annual Ceremony of Washing the Lions' at the Tower, dated April Fool's Day 1857! The records also moved, to the Public Record Office in Chancery Lane. But the Crown Jewels and the collection of armour remained, visited by more and more people each year.

During the First and Second World Wars the Tower was used as a prison again. Between 1914 and 1916 eleven German spies were executed there by firing squad. In 1978 members of the Royal Family visited the Tower to honour its 900th anniversary. The picture opposite shows the Tower as it looks today.

THE TOWER RESTORED. This is the architect, Sir Christopher Wren, who rebuilt St. Paul's Cathedral after the Fire of London. He was Surveyor General at the Tower and was called in to provide space for more prisoners after the 'Glorious Revolution' of 1688. Wren also repaired the White Tower and took away its Norman appearance by making most of the windows larger.

ESCAPE DISGUISED AS A WOMAN. This is the wife of a Scottish rebel, the fifth Earl of Nithsdale. On the eve of his execution in 1716, Lady Nithsdale visited him at the Tower. She brought in make-up and a wig, and a friend wearing two sets of clothes. Nithsdale escaped dressed as a woman, weeping loudly into a handkerchief. The guards thought they could hear his voice in the cell, but that was his wife; she was talking to herself and imitating his voice as best she could.

NEWTON AND THE MINT. The famous scientist, Sir Isaac Newton, was Master of the Mint from 1699 to 1727. In Newton's time, machines like these for making coins were used instead of hammers. It was very

hard work swinging the lead weights to push the dies together. A new set of coins was made using these methods, and all the old coins were taken out of circulation.

THE SOUVENIR HUNTER. Lord Coningsby was proud of his short imprisonment. You can see the Tower in the background of this portrait. While at the Tower he somehow managed to order a gun for himself from the workshops there. It had this rhyme engraved on it:

I in the Tower became a gun,
    in seventeen hundred and twenty-one.
Earl Coningsby, a prisoner there,
    bespoke and took me to his care.

ANSON'S TREASURE. In 1744 excited crowds watched this long line of wagons bringing captured Spanish treasure worth £500,000 to the Tower. Commodore George Anson had lost five of his six ships in the fight with Spain. But the sixth ship captured the Spanish prize ship *Nostra Senora de Covadonga*, which was full of treasure.

SIMON FRASER, LORD LOVAT. The last prisoner to die by the axe at the Tower was Lord Lovat. He told the Lieutenant of the Tower that it was not he but his eldest son who had supported Bonny Prince Charlie's uprising in 1745. 'We can hang my eldest son, and then my second son will be my heir and can marry your daughter', the wily old man suggested as a last hope. He still lost his head. The scenes above were sketched by Hogarth at Lord Lovat's trial.

THE FREEDOM OF THE PRESS. John Wilkes, a member of Parliament, was arrested in 1763 for writing against King George III. He was taken to the Tower but later released. Later, in 1771, he defended the freedom of the Press, when the Lord Mayor and an Alderman were imprisoned in the Tower for publishing reports of Parliament's debates. Here you can see angry crowds supporting him on his way to the Tower. The Prime Minister's coach was smashed to pieces in the rioting.

AN AMERICAN IN THE TOWER. This is Henry
Laurens, who was President of the American Con-
gress in 1777–8. He was captured at sea on his way
to Holland to seek support for the new United States
of America in the fight for independence. The warders at the Tower greeted him by singing 'Yankee
Doodle'. Back in America he liked to be called 'Tower'
Laurens.

THE FIRE OF 1841. The Tower had escaped the
Great Fire of 1666. The worst fire in the Tower itself
was in 1841. The Crown Jewels were saved, as you
can see opposite, but William and Mary's great
Armoury building was destroyed.

RESTORING THE TOWER. The Duke of Wellington was Constable of the Tower from 1826 to 1852. Wellington used the burned-out site of the Armoury for more building. Here you can see the foundation stone

being laid for the Waterloo Barracks, named after his great victory over Napoleon in 1815. Restoration of the Tower continued after Wellington's death, and more buildings were opened to the public.

MUSEUM. In the nineteenth and twentieth centuries more and more people began to visit the Tower. In 1978 over three million visitors came to the Tower. They admired the Crown Jewels, now kept deep underground, and questioned 'beefeaters' like this one about the legend that the Tower will fall if the Tower ravens leave it. A Raven Master takes great care to feed them well!

WORLD WAR I. This *Punch* cartoon of 1916 suggests that one cure for the shortage of arms might be to use the crossbows from the Tower Armoury. Eleven German spies were tried and executed by firing squad at the Tower in the First World War. The Tower came under attack in a new way — by Zeppelin airship. The nearest bomb landed in the moat, but did little damage.

HITLER'S DEPUTY. Here you can see Rudolf Hess and his wife. Hess was deputy leader of the Nazi party in Germany and flew single-handed to England to try and make peace on his own. However, he did

not succeed and was imprisoned in the Tower for a short time. After the war he was sent back to Germany to spend the rest of his life in prison. In 1966 he became the only prisoner at Spandau jail.

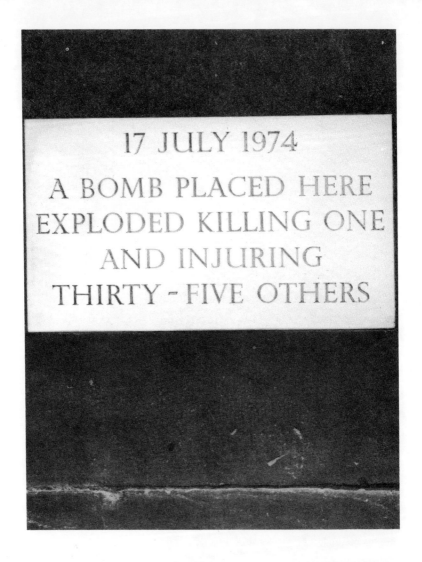

17 JULY 1974

A BOMB PLACED HERE
EXPLODED KILLING ONE
AND INJURING
THIRTY - FIVE OTHERS

900 YEARS ON. In 1974 an Irish Republican Army bomb exploded in the White Tower. One person died and others, including children, were injured. Once again innocent children suffered there, as the little princes had done centuries before. In 1978 the Tower celebrated its 900th anniversary, with royal visits and jubilant crowds. Two strands in the Tower's grand history — pageantry and violence — came together once again.

New Words

Abdication	Giving up the Throne.
Ambassador	Minister who is sent to a foreign country to represent his own country.
Beefeater	Name given to the Yeomen Warders at the Tower.
Curtain wall	Wall round a castle which connects the towers.
Die	Engraved stamp for making a pattern, as on coins.
Drawbridge	Bridge hinged at one end which can be quickly drawn up to stop people crossing.
Executioner	Man whose job it is to put criminals to death.
Keep	The central building in a castle which is often the living quarters.
Menagerie	Collection of caged wild animals.
Mint	Place where coins are made.
Observatory	Building with telescopes for watching the stars and planets.
Ordnance	Store where guns and ammunition are kept.
Portcullis	Metal grating which can be let down quickly to close a gateway.
Rack	Instrument of torture which stretched the victim's limbs.
Ransom	Money paid in return for the release of a captive.
Scavenger's daughter	Instrument of torture which doubled the victim up in an iron squeezing device.
Yeoman Warder	Title given to the forty ex-soldiers who guard the Tower.

Date Chart

1078   The Normans began building the Tower in stone.

1190s   Richard I built a curtain wall round the Keep.

1230s   Henry III built a Royal Palace at the Tower. The royal menagerie was first housed at the Tower.

1300s   Edward I surrounded the Tower with an outer wall.

1381   The Tower was invaded by rebels during the Peasants' Revolt.

1483   Young Princes disappeared from the Tower.

1500s   Henry VII set up a royal bodyguard, known as the Yeomen of the Guard.

1509   Henry VIII became king. He strengthened the Tower and built a new Ordnance.

1554   Lady Jane Grey executed at the Tower.

1605   Gunpowder Plot discovered — Guy Fawkes arrested and brought to the Tower.

1649   Charles I executed after the Civil War. Oliver Cromwell sold many of the Crown Jewels.

1660   Charles II became king, and ordered new Crown Jewels to be made.

1680s   Christopher Wren renovated much of the Tower.

1747   Lord Lovat executed. He was the last prisoner to die by the axe at the Tower.

1841   Part of the Tower destroyed by fire.

1840s   Much of the Tower repaired and more buildings opened to the public.

1900s   Tower becomes one of London's main tourist attractions.

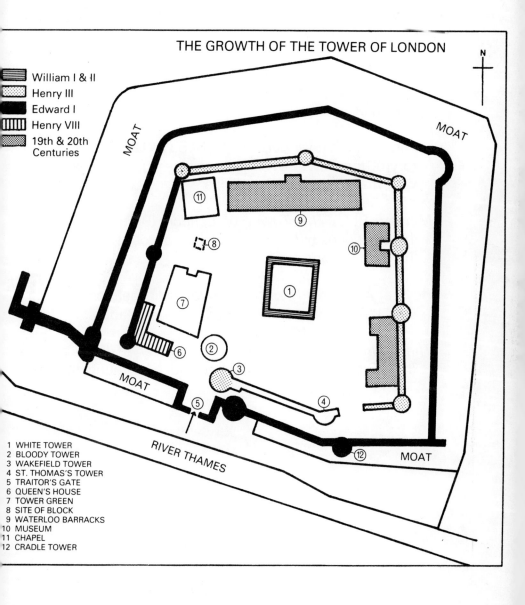

THE GROWTH OF THE TOWER OF LONDON

N

William I & II
Henry III
Edward I
Henry VIII
19th & 20th
Centuries

MOAT
MOAT
MOAT
MOAT

RIVER THAMES

1 WHITE TOWER
2 BLOODY TOWER
3 WAKEFIELD TOWER
4 ST. THOMAS'S TOWER
5 TRAITOR'S GATE
6 QUEEN'S HOUSE
7 TOWER GREEN
8 SITE OF BLOCK
9 WATERLOO BARRACKS
10 MUSEUM
11 CHAPEL
12 CRADLE TOWER

More Books

Borg, A. (ed) *Strange Stories from the Tower of London* (Historical Times Ltd., 1976). Stories of some of the less well-known incidents that have happened at the Tower.

Dobson, J. *Children of the Tower* (Heinemann, 1978). True stories about some of the children who have stayed at the Tower.

Hammond, P. *Royal Fortress* (H.M.S.O., 1978). A history of the Tower over the last nine hundred years with many colour photographs.

Minney, R. J. *The Tower of London* (Prentice-Hall, 1970). Long but very readable account of the Tower's history.

Rowse, A. L. *The Tower of London* (Michael Joseph, 1977). A history of the Tower for older readers.

The Young Visitor's Guide to the Tower of London (H.M.S.O., 1974). A good book to take round the Tower with you.

Index

Picture acknowledgements

British Museum, 12, 36, 41; Department of the Environment, 11, 15, 16, 17, 19, 30, 48—9, 52, 56, 72, 78, 90; Mansell Collection, 88—9; Mary Evans Picture Library, *frontispiece*, 14, 32—3, 40—41, 43, 50, 51, 71, 75, 81, 82, 84—5, 86; Museum of London, 6, 8—9, 10, 42, 68—9; National Portrait Gallery, 57, 66; Peter Newark's Historical Pictures, *jacket picture*; Radio Times Hulton Picture Library, 79; Rediffusion Television Limited, 54, 55; Royal Mint, 76—7. The pictures on pages 22, 24, 28, 31, 34, 44, 45, 47, 61, 64—5, 67, 83, 87 were provided by the author. The plan on page 93 was drawn by Celia Packham-Head. All other pictures are taken from the Wayland Picture Library.